Love Doesn't Die reminds us all that everyone is a divine being who comes to life on earth with a spiritual purpose. Our self perceptions are created over time and are shaped by successes and failures and how we handle them.

"What we think about ourselves plays a great role in what we actually become."

"I unfortunately have never met Yorke Brent-Harris. I feel as if I know him. His compassion, spontaneous, intellect, enthusiasm, humor, patience, calmness, spirituality and sharing of his life experiences and family history should serve as a role model to us all allowing us to be the best we can be to all who we meet and to our future generations."

Ronald Valmore Lucier – Pranic Healer

LOVE DOESN'T DIE

LOVE DOESN'T DIE

ANGELA BRENT-HARRIS

OPEN BOOK
EDITIONS
A Berrett–Koehler Partner

Love Doesn't Die

iUniverse books may be ordered through booksellers or by contacting:

iUniverse
1663 Liberty Drive
Bloomington, IN 47403
www.iuniverse.com
1-800-Authors (1-800-288-4677)

ISBN: 978-1-4759-3452-6 (sc)
ISBN: 978-1-4759-3451-9 (e)

Library of Congress Control Number: 2012911315

Printed in the United States of America

iUniverse rev. date: 08/14/2012

I dedicate this book as a tribute to my loving dad,
Yorke Devere Brent-Harris, who always supported me
in every endeavor. He taught me how to find happiness
in everything, to be kind, optimistic, and that colossal
things are instinctive from glimmers of inspiration.

I also dedicate this book to my mom, Hope Fay
Brent-Harris, for her infinite love, kindness, devotion,
and for her endless support and her selflessness.

Introduction

— ◆ —

I will take you on a magical journey of memories of my dad that will stay alive in my heart forever. When I think of how he touched my life, the first word that comes to mind is *admiration*. Although I could make a much longer list, I would like to share just a few of the reasons I admired my dad, who was a real old-fashioned gentleman.

First, I admired my dad's love and commitment to my mom, and not just marital commitment. He was committed to making her happy!

It was important to her, and so it became important to him. They were happily married for forty-eight years, and during his last days, his only concern was for my mom's well-being, and not his own impending mortality.

I also admired him for the kind of father he was to my brother, sister, and me. Yes, he loved us very much. But he also instilled in us a core value system that defined who he was. *That* was a man who kept promises. He honored commitment. He was a man of integrity.

Whenever we stumbled, he fully expected us to see things through, all the way to the end and without drama. He would say to me, "I believe in you, and you can do it." It's strange to talk in the past tense about a person who knew me through and through, nurturing and supporting all my dreams throughout my entire life. I'm trying to focus on being grateful to have had so many years with Daddy instead of being confounded by the thought of the rest of my life without him.

We were like planets orbiting around him as a sun. Not many can match the brilliance of the combination of his mind and spirit.

He used his brain and his heart. He attracted our attention and emulation, as he did with most who met him.

Our family activities whirled around his gravitational pull as he taught, advised, teased, and cheered us on.

As with all charismatic figures, his strength radiated into his flaws with equal volume. When he intended to annoy or criticize, he really succeeded. When tired, he demanded to be waited on like a real Jamaican father. It's hard to summarize the spectrum of a life so extraordinarily rich and full.

**Photo of my mom and dad sharing
their wedding cake**

The Flavor of My Family

Yorke Devere Brent-Harris, my dad, was the fourth child and second son of Wilford and Estella Brent-Harris, from a family of four boys and three girls. He was born in Mount Providence, Clarendon, Jamaica, on November 23, 1934.

He married my mom, Hope Fay Tucker of Montego Bay, on April 28, 1962, and this loving union yielded son Andre Brent-Harris, whose life got shortened in 1992, and two daughters, Yvette Brent-Harris and me—Angela Brent-Harris.

I will appease your appetite with a taste of the lovely people in my family. My dad was a man of determination. He was venturesome and very positive in his opinions, so when he knew a thing to be right, it was almost impossible to move him. He was just and honest and loved with vigor and passion. My dad was a lover of classical and semiclassical music and a jazz enthusiast, and he promoted

My dad is at the front left end standing beside 2 of his 3 brothers in his childhood family portrait

several jazz concerts in Kingston and Montego Bay. He played the violin as a youngster. He was an Anglican in 1949 at Kingston Chapel, where he was a member of the school choir.

He was a member of the St. James Parish church, and secretary of its Brotherhood of St. Andrew chapter. He was a member of Eckankar, the Scottish Free Masons, and the Elgin Lodge, where he was director of ceremonies, and a justice of the peace. He was the first president of the Paradise Acres Citizens Association of Montego Bay and served as its president three times, and he was a member of the Orchid Society in Montego Bay, Jamaica.

My mom is a woman of exotic and infinite beauty. She has endured a lot in life, and she still manages to overcome any obstacle. I often wish I had her strength and perseverance. She is spiritualistic, idealistic, and religious. She is an incredible entertainer and enjoys society. She is sincere, honest, and frank, and she is a very loyal friend. My mom has a green thumb; if she plants as much as a frail leaf in the dirt, it will flourish and grow. She is a lover of orchids and exotic plants and flowers. She craves art and loves antique artifacts. She is an ardent collector of Lladro and Lalique crystals.

My sister, Yvette, has a great deal of personal pride yet likes to command. Her passions are deep, and she loves with intensity. Yvette can lose control of her emotions easily and oftentimes acts hastily when excited. However, she quickly regains her better judgment and makes amends. She tries to put on a tough façade sometimes, but beneath all that, she is shy, curious, gentle, and mushy. She is also conscientious and very reliable.

My brother, Andre, was scrupulously honest and faithful to duty. He was sincere and said just what he meant. He was an intellectual, a clear, keen thinker, and a lucid talker. He had a big heart and was very generous. He made it easy for everyone to love him, and he was admired by all.

As for me, I was born with a kind heart. I can be rather quiet and reserved, yet fun-loving with a strange sense of humor. Not everyone understands my jokes.

I am gentle and affectionate and always strive to add to the happiness of my loved ones. I am very humble and very kind. I have a keen and alert mind and much executive ability. I am also spiritualistic like my parents. I believe our purpose on this earth is to find our way back to God.

My childhood family photo. I am in my mom's lap.

Humble Heritage

———— ·•◆•· ————

I was born and raised in Montego Bay, Jamaica. I savored and enjoyed every moment and have no regrets. Jamaica is the ravishingly beautiful sunshine island. Jamaica is oftentimes referred to as a cultural superpower. I think this is mainly because the culture and reggae music is world renowned. Reggae music is the most internationally known facet of Jamaican culture, which was brought to worldwide popularity by the "Reggae ambassador," Rastafarian Bob Marley. Reggae originated as what was called Rock Steady and Ska of the 1950s and 1960s and continues to evolve. The heartfelt lyrics of Bob Marley are just a preview into the strong oral tradition of Jamaica. Storytelling and folk tales permeate the teaching of morals and values; for generations the popular folk hero has been Anansi, an African spider, who shows all aspects of human frailties and strength through cunning behavior and charming wit.

Jamaica is the third largest island and is one of the larger set of islands referred to as the Greater Antilles. To me, Jamaica is like an enormous fruit salad, because its rich and vibrant culture is derived from descendants of African slaves who were brought to Jamaica in the late seventeenth to early nineteenth century, combined with descendants from East Indians, Chinese, Arabs, and Europeans. I think the best thing is to see a Jamaican who looks Chinese speaking Jamaican patois and saying, "Yeah, mon!" It cracks me up all the time. Surely, this gives beautiful harmony and meaning to the national motto, "Out of Many, One People."

I have to say that Jamaica is indeed the enchanting jewel of the Caribbean. Well, you see, there are pristine, aquamarine beaches caressing the sugary white sands. There are the crystal-clear rivers and majestic, cascading waterfalls, rapturous sunsets, lush trails of tropical flora, beautiful and breathtaking mountain peaks, many charming greathouses, and the cool sea breezes that tease and tantalize you with the sensual beat of reggae and the rhythm of the heartbeat of the people with large smiles and love of life. Panoramas of sea and mountains are on every side of beautiful Jamaica. Countless coastal roads boast magnificent views of mountain streams that splash down in silvery sprays of gushing waterfalls, rushing toward the sea. Jamaica is definitely the land of perpetual summer. The island knows no winter. The seasonal rain causes the vegetation to be lush and plentiful. It certainly is sufficient to help nature's task of preserving and distributing the splendor of the land.

The beauty of the island mixed with the sweetness of the people has imbued the island with a wonderfully happy atmosphere. What can I say? Every time I return to Jamaica for a vacation, I simply cannot resist the allure of paradise, because I know that I am going home to a magical utopia. The people may not have everything they want, but they are smiling and happy. Jamaica is a place where you go and have strangers helping you push-start a car, and everyone is smiling with not a worry in the world. Jamaicans are in love with life, and it is written all over their faces. It gives you a natural high just to absorb the sweet energy of contentment from the people. The friendly and warm spirit of the people is evident in their ready smiles and the ever-popular slogan "no problem" that characterizes the happy-go-lucky and easy Jamaican attitude.

Now, the food is another story altogether. Jamaican cuisine is a delicious fusion of spices, various meats, tropical fruits, and vegetables, which creates an enticing, tasty, and tempting meal. The national dish is *ackee* and saltfish, and some other popular dishes are jerk chicken, peppered shrimp, and curried goat to name a few. Ackee is actually a vegetable that grows in a red pod on trees. The edible portion is light yellow in color.

Love Blossoms

As I close my eyes, I can vividly remember that I was a very happy little girl. Nothing really seemed to bother me. I was the youngest of three children and quite a little comedienne.

My parents would have occasional social gatherings at home with their friends. They loved to entertain. I can look back now and realize why I didn't become much of a smoker or drinker. It's mostly because alcohol, cigarettes, and even marijuana weren't taboo for me while growing up. My dad would drink an icy cold beer, namely Jamaican Red Stripe or Heineken, mostly on the weekends. My brother, sister, and I would watch the bottle curiously as Daddy poured the golden beer into a big clear mug. It fascinated me when the beer hissed and foamed up at the top. I thought that was the coolest sight, especially if some crept down the side of the mug. My sister would always be the first to jump up into Daddy's lap and beg

This is me when I was about 6 years old

him sweetly for a taste of the beer, and he would let her try it. She liked the taste of beer. I would taste a little, but I disliked the bitter taste even though I liked the robust and yeasty scent. I would tell myself quietly that the beer needed some sugar and perhaps some lemon juice too to give it the perfect taste. Christmastime was also a treat because we were allowed to taste red wine, blush, or sherry. I remember smacking my lips when I tasted the sweet and tangy sherry that stained my lips.

The traditional Jamaican Christmas pudding was another story in itself. It was a dark fruitcake made with prunes and raisins and soaked with rum, and I could practically get a buzz from eating just a small slice. Then there was the traditional sorrel beverage that was as red as blood. Sorrel is not to be confused with the vegetable of the same name from temperate countries. Sorrel is a favorite West Indian drink at Christmas and New Year. Actually, it's more of a spiced iced tea, as the juice is drawn from the red sepals of the roselle plant (Hibiscus sabdariffa), which is commonly called sorrel in the Caribbean. This drink is a favorite with children, who are often given the task of picking sorrel by removing the red sepals from the prickly seed. The drink is prepared in two batches, with one batch being spiked with rum for the adults. The drink usually needs a lot of sugar to temper the tartness of the fruit, but to my mind it should not be made thick and sweet, for then it becomes sickly and cloying. The sorrel had a very sweet yet gingery flavor with a distinct tart taste spiced with overproof Jamaican white rum. I often thought that it could have been easy for me to become an alcoholic.

Sorrel is also known to be a sedative, a diuretic, and a tonic. It is used as a remedy for cancer and blood pressure. To me, sorrel is nature's own noncarbonated soft drink. This drink is never too sweet or syrupy. Well, my home where I grew up had an authentic and beautifully wooden carved liquor trolley that boasted all kinds of liqueurs, all types of rums, and scotch, tonics, and whiskey to name a few.

I must say that my sister and brother and I sampled almost all of them, and I would hit my head because some were so potent and made my eyes spin. My dad also kept a gorgeous adorned silver box in the living room that was filled with cigarettes. The box looked like a pretty little trinket box. My dad would offer cigarettes to guests whenever my parents entertained.

I think I was about nine years old when I was very curious about cigarettes and wanted to try smoking one. Sure enough, I sneaked and lighted one up, and I puffed on it, coughed, and gasped and choked profusely. As a child I had major sinus problems, and lo and behold the cigarettes caused my sinuses to flare up. I thought I was going to have a heart attack. I vowed from that day never to mess around with cigarettes again. That was quite a scary experience for me.

Weekends

———◆◆◆———

The weekends were the best times with Daddy. It was a real treat for me and for my family. I will share my favorite times with you.

I can remember clearly when I was a little girl, waking up on the weekends to sweet melodies of soothing jazz that filled the air. I learned that jazz is a musical tradition and style of music that originated at the beginning of the twentieth century. It treats the basic elements common to other music in a unique way. To me, jazz was a language of harmony, melody, and rhythm. It differed according to the musicians' styles and temperaments.

Let me tell you more. I would run to the family room to find my dad marinating in the jazz rhythms as he swayed his head with his eyes gently closed while tapping his feet to the beat. He always seemed to be in a trance with jazz. For sure he knew I was standing there, because he would open one eye to look at me, and he would smile

Photo of dad in the 70's

and I would giggle. That was all I needed to jump right up in his lap. I was so amazed by his love for jazz. It was definitely one of his favorite pastimes. I would close my eyes and try to figure out which instruments were playing.

Hmm, I heard flutes, trombones, bass, piano, guitars, drums, clarinet, saxophones, maracas, tuba, and trumpets galore. I was happier than a clam just trying to figure out this sweet mystical jazz that would go on for hours. When I gazed out the window, I saw all kinds of birds and brightly colored butterflies parading in motions to the jazz. Even the bees were dancing, and the majestic dragonflies seemed to have an orchestra of their own.

The leaves on the trees were not left out either, because they were bopping around in a sweeping motion to the rhythm of the jazz.

I believed that Mommy's flowers in the garden— orchids, roses, anthuriums, hibiscus, and other tropical flowers in abundance—certainly enjoyed Daddy's jazz music, and it showed. They definitely looked healthier than the regular plants, and the flowers grew bigger blooms too. They responded well to the jazz music, and it sure seemed like they were hypnotized, stimulated, and revitalized by the beat and the tune. This would be an amazing science experiment if it were put to the test.

Some holidays or long weekends were also a rare treat. My dad would buy a fifty-pound block of ice at the ice factory downtown. Mommy would be waiting with a variety of flavored syrups for this wonderful experience. Soon Daddy would arrive. He placed the ice on a big table out in the backyard. Then we would invite all the neighborhood children to be part of the excitement. We would each be able to shave our own icy delight. The ice shaver was a hand ice plane made from rustproof cast-aluminum construction with a hinged cover. We made cool, refreshing ice the old-fashioned way (not like today) by passing the shaver over the ice several times until the shaver was filled. We would then empty the shaved ice into Mommy's cute enamel goblets that she had for each of us. The shaved ice wasn't crunchy at all! It was very light and fluffy, like snow. We would add whatever flavored syrups we fancied to our refreshing shaved ice to make it sweet or tangy. The amazing thing at that time was that you wouldn't hear any talking, just a lot of slurping.

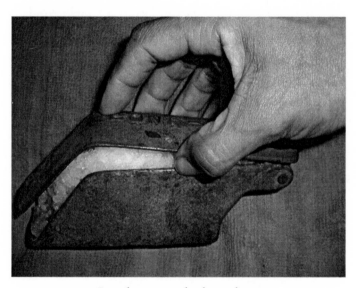

Ice shaver with shaved ice

Daddy's Field Trips

———◆◆◆———

Then there were Daddy's field trips. Oh yes! I was a curious little girl and wanted to know about anything and everything. All I had to do was ask Daddy, and for sure the answers to my questions would come alive. I remember my fascination with the sweet golden brown sugar crystals. "Daddy, where does sugar come from?" I asked.

That's all it took, and I felt like I was ready for an adventure on the Magic School Bus. Before I knew it, I was packed up and ready with the family to go on a mission to find out where sugar came from. Off we went for a long drive in the car with a scenic view of the lavish green mountains on one side and the brilliant blue ocean on the other. I thought they knew what was happening, because the waves greeted the sandy shore as if to share my happiness. To my excitement, I soon arrived at the great big Appleton Estate Sugar Factory in a warm, lush setting full of colorful tropical flowers, green grass, and gorgeous peacocks in a town called Siloah, where Daddy grew up.

His parents, who were both elementary school principals for many years, also grew up in Siloah.

I had the time of my life. We had a tour guide show us around. A man with a donkey showed how they used to use donkeys to turn the machine that ground the sugarcane at this 100-year-old donkey-driven cane mill. WOW!

Sugarcane stalks grow from old stalks planted in the ground. When their growing season is over, (after seven to twenty-two months) and the stalks are seven to fifteen feet tall, they are cut and taken to a sugar mill.

At the Sugar Estates, machines wash, cut, and shred the stalks into a pulpy mass. With water continually sprayed on it, this pulpy mass is crushed between rollers to squeeze out the sugary juice, called cane juice. The liquid, now a dark grayish-green color, is heated to its boiling point, and chemicals are added to remove impurities.

Next, the juice is placed in huge tanks to evaporate, leaving thick syrup. This syrup is heated to remove more and more water until crystals form.

These crystals must be separated from the syrup, so they are put into a centrifuge machine, which spins it around rapidly.

The sugar that is left inside the machine's cylinders is called raw sugar. Then it is dissolved, treated with chemicals, filtered, crystallized once more, and allowed to solidify, this time into golden brown sugar and then pure white sugar. Wow! This reminded me of Willy Wonka's Chocolate Factory, except instead of chocolate, you were able to sample fresh cane juice, molasses, and wet sugar with a sophisticated flavor and rich aroma. Now I knew where sugar came from.

It did not end there. Another time I asked, "Daddy, what causes the bubbles and fizz in soda?" Uh-oh! I think ght. I was soon on my way to another one ld trips, this time to the soda factory to caused bubbles and fizz in soda.

er that I was able to sample all different . I loved cream soda the most. It was clear th just a hint of vanilla. The grape- and d sodas were yummy too! Here is what I learned about sodas. First, you need treated water or spring water. Second, you need your variety of flavored syrup. The water is then evacuated of all oxygen. Then the water and syrup are precisely blended together at about 2.5–3 parts water to 1 part syrup (depending on the type of soda) and blasted with carbon dioxide, which causes the bubbles and fizz. Then it is sent to a filler and fills cans or bottles.

The wildest trip was when I asked, "Daddy, where does aluminum foil come from?" Goodness gracious! Off I went on an exploration on one of Daddy's field trips. It would be one that I would never forget. I remember the drive being so long that I even drifted off to sleep.

Not long afterward, we arrived at a huge gate. The area was surrounded by reddish dirt everywhere. On top of the gate was a big sign with "Bauxite Factory" written on top. I could not pronounce it right, so Daddy helped me. It didn't make sense to me. What does bauxite have to do with aluminum? Of course I would soon find out. Aluminum is the third most plentiful element on earth and can be found in rocks, plants, and animals. It is mined from the earth's surface and is always mixed with other elements. Bauxite, the name for aluminum ore, is separated by electrical currents and turned into foil.

Love Blooms

————◆————

Daddy was always consistent with who he was, even during my teenage years. However, both of my parents were strict disciplinarians. Whenever we broke a rule or did something against their wishes, it was a guarantee that we would get a spanking. My mom would quote the Bible, saying, "He that spareth his rod hateth his son: but he that loveth him chasteneth him betimes" (Proverbs 13:24). This actually meant that if you do not punish children when they do something wrong, they will not learn what is right. I went to an all-girls high school, and I have to say that I rarely if ever saw anyone being disrespectful or curt. The schools in Jamaica didn't joke at all when it came to discipline. Also we had to wear uniforms that always looked immaculate as well as socks and loafers. The law granted the school permission to physically punish the children if they broke rules.

The boys' high school was a little different. The boys

wore khaki uniform shirts with epaulettes and long pants. If a boy broke a rule and was disrespectful, he would be sent to the principal's office to receive caning on his derriere, and the number of strokes depended on the rule he had broken. Speaking of boys, my sister and I were cautious about having boyfriends, and didn't have serious boyfriends until we graduated from high school.

My mom instilled the fear of God in us that if we as much as looked at a boy's thigh, we would become pregnant. So, guess what? Surely we lost interest there. We were brought up then in a society that believed in marriage before sex.

I remember as a teenager, walking on the beaches of Jamaica and finding tiny marijuana plants growing in the sand. I would pull off some of the leaves and take them home and press them and display them in my photo album for fun. I didn't have much desire to try marijuana, especially after the cigarette experience I had had. However, I went twice to a Jamaican Reggae Sunsplash concert by the ocean, and I clearly remember the singer throwing a big *spliff,* which is a rolled-up marijuana cigar. To my amazement, the crowd of people dispersed and dove while almost trampling each other just to get it.

The smoke from the people in the audience who were smoking marijuana was so thick that it formed huge clouds above our heads. I went home with my head feeling as big as a watermelon, and I was in a daze just from inhaling the smoke. I woke up the next day with a ghastly fever and intense headache. I knew then that just wasn't for me. All those temptations were there while growing up, but it wasn't taboo, and maybe that's why it wasn't a big deal for me. That is why when I was seventeen and went to the University of South Carolina to study, I was focused. The alcohol and other things weren't taboo for me.

I truly think that Jamaica is the only place where there was no drinking age back then, and you could see a six-year-old going to the store to buy beer or alcohol.

Dad's Coolness

M y father's strength was a quiet one, defined primarily by his unfailing ability to rise above his limitations in a never-ending effort to serve those around him. He was an intensely private man who nonetheless spent a lifetime actively seeking out and playing roles in the community that forced from him great levels of personal interaction with others. We were lucky to spend our lives with one of the rare ones. My dad was funny and compassionate and welcoming and spontaneous and so intelligent. He loved social gatherings, and read voraciously.

One of his greatest traits was his calmness and patience. He never let anything or anyone bother him. He was just plain cool and easy. Anytime my mom asked him to do anything, he would just answer, "Yes, dear, I'm running." He aimed to please her.

Whenever we wanted something as children or needed

permission to go somewhere and we asked Daddy, he would always say, "Ask your mom, and whatever she says is my answer too."

Daddy participated in activities that I enjoyed. It could be something as simple as raking up the leaves in the yard or cooking a special dish together. We created some scrumptious and delicious meals together such as curried chicken, shrimp lo mein, and lobster Thermidor. We enjoyed playing a card game too. We usually sat on the verandah in comfy chairs and played Old Maid, where you remove three of the queens from the deck. The main goal is to avoid being the player holding the Old Maid—the remaining queen—at the end of the game. We also played Sevens. The game of Sevens is so much fun, and it is very simple. Three to seven players can enjoy this game. The goal is to be the first player to lay down all the cards in one suit from seven to ace or eight to king; this suit system is followed in many solitaire games. The game begins with each player being dealt seven cards. The game proceeds clockwise, with each player playing his or her turn or passing. If the number of players is not even, the number of cards distributed will not be equal.

To make this equal the extra cards can be placed face-up in the center, used later by any player wishing to use them. On each turn, no card can be played on a seven until the eight is also played, but a seven can be played any time. If the seven and eight are played, the next card has to follow suit and be a six or nine. If a player does not have this card, he or she passes, but if the player does hold the card, he or she has to play it. Players may use tactics to change the direction of the game or to better their own game. Children as well as adults can enjoy this game, as it is easy to play but interesting as well if strategy is used properly. One of the tactical moves a player can make is to hold back a card that is the highest or lowest of a particular suit, forcing other players to play cards in the blocking player's suit of choice. This can be achieved because the players with higher or lower cards than what the person blocking the game has will not be able to play any other card in between. We had so much fun!

We also enjoyed going to religious services. Jamaica is a very religious and predominantly Christian society comprising various denominations: Anglican, Methodist, Baptist, Seventh-day Adventist, Pentecostal, Catholic, and Rastafarian. Anyway, we would go to the Anglican service with my dad since he was Anglican and my mom is Catholic.

We loved going to see movies. The first movie I ever saw with my parents was *King Kong,* and we saw *Jaws* and *Star Wars* on other occasions.

Sometimes it was interesting to sit and listen to quotes about life that my dad shared with me. Even spending an afternoon running errands together was a real treat. Sometimes he would go to the post office, to the bank, or to pick up stationery. My dad would also sit with me and tell me stories about his life. I loved to hear him tell his stories. This was a tradition he grew up with in his childhood—listening while his relatives gathered for a lively evening of eating, debating, and telling tall tales.

Jamaicans' gift of storytelling and finding humor in life's challenges has always been the foundation for rich and dynamic theater. There is always a production for one to enjoy, not to mention the national Jamaican Pantomime, which blends comedy and music to create a thrilling and charming theater experience.

Treasured Moments

———◆◆◆———

Being a family man blossomed into a lifetime passion for Daddy. He made a wise decision to choose a wife with common sense. She gave him a grounded traditional home from which he could pull his practical jokes without spinning out of control.

It was always a balancing act to keep his jokes from going too far. Probably his sense of humor is what he'll be remembered for the most. I'd love to hear a compilation of all the jokes he told and all the practical jokes he participated in or instigated. It would be a long list.

He would tell involved stories about his adventures, or weave historical scenarios and explain how they related to our lives today. Of course, he always laughed loudest and longest at his own jokes, with a big grin and wiggling eyebrows and his shoulders shaking. We got to hear those jokes repeated over and over if we showed appreciation for them.

Wedding photo of my mom and dad

One of the finest features Daddy possessed was his enthusiasm. Everything was "the best" in his view. Every steak he grilled and every single batch of chop suey he'd proclaim was "the best I've ever made!" Every drawing I drew or poem I wrote was a miracle of genius, according to Daddy.

Keeping files on each child, he knew the fluctuations of our personalities and feelings or needs. We've discussed this: each of us kids secretly suspected that we were his favorite at some point. And I think we each *really* were, in the same way that each steak was the best he ever made. Each child really was the best he ever made. Although not given to public displays of affection, he slowly and with great sincerity became a hugger in later life, welcoming extended family over the years, a daughter-in-law, sons-in-law, all those grandchildren, nieces and nephews.

Daddy lived a life of quiet inspiration. He loved working out at the gym and keeping in great shape. I remember that he told me to focus on what is most important and meaningful in life. One day he told me the story of two men in a prison cell gazing through a window; one saw the mud and the other saw the stars. Dad emphasized that success in life depends on how you perceive life. He would tell me that what you think of yourself plays a great role in what you actually become. Self-perception is created over time from the environment and other people around you. As you grow, it is also shaped by the successes and the failures that you face and the manner in which you treat them. A person who is self-confident faces negative situations optimistically and looks at them as consequences of certain factors that may be external and internal. He does not believe that the new additions to his negative outcome are products of his capabilities alone. This enables the optimistic person to strive to overcome the hurdles that he faces going forward in life. A pessimistic person tends to blame himself for all the defeats and setbacks and gets wrought with thoughts of failure, refusing to try to work around problems. A positive approach will also ensure that your self-image, self-esteem, and confidence experience a major boost.

The one manner in which you can ensure that your mind entertains only positive thoughts is to talk to yourself. Try to speak to yourself and initiate a meaningful dialogue that motivates you to think and act positively.

Spiritual Wonderment

My dad's life was worth emulating, with its great faith, spirituality, generosity, and simple joys. My dad couldn't walk down a street without whistling, couldn't pass a stranger without saying "hello." He couldn't see a need without reaching in his pocket. He always told us that if we couldn't say something good about someone, it was better to not say anything at all. Of course, that reminded me of Thumper, a fictional rabbit character from Disney's animated movie *Bambi* who sings a little song about that same subject.

The greatest pain for my parents was when my brother passed away from an accident in 1992. My dad took his death to heart and grieved privately. Neither of my parents was ever the same person after that. I think the hardest thing in life is for parents to outlive their children.

As I became older, I saw a lot of my father in myself. I always thought that I was rich, not in monetary wealth but in being content. I was happy with who I was despite the problems and obstacles along the way. I was thankful for family, and for having a roof over my head, clothes to wear, food to eat, and a job, and that was all that mattered. I became more spiritually aware as I got older. I connected with my dad in that sense too. I grew up in the Catholic religion, but in my late thirties, I became interested in Buddhism, heights of meditation, aromatherapy, and the healing effect of crystals. I didn't take these spiritual teachings lightly; I began to learn more by studying the things I was curious about and later became a Reiki master and a crystal (chakra) healer.

I shared this with my dad, but he would only smile and say that I was just beginning spiritually. He would say, "Chirpie, before I leave this earth, I will teach you all you need to know." My dad called me Chirpie because he said that I was always happy-go-lucky, and that I never seemed to be bothered by anything. He compared me to a happy little bird, chirping and soaring through the sky.

My dad's religion was Anglican, which is like Protestant, and my mom was Catholic. However, during the late 1960s, my dad became an ECKist, which is a member of Eckankar or coworker with God. It's very interesting, because he remained an Anglican and was very involved in the church, but he also was an ECKist.

Surrounded by Love and Light

In September 2003, I had a near-death experience at my home in Boca Raton, Florida. It was a beautiful morning, around nine o'clock. The air was fresh and crisp, the sun was in its glory, and even the birds were singing. The air conditioner had stopped working. I knew right away that the unit in the attic, which was right above the garage, was clogged again and filled with water. My mom was right outside the opened garage door with my sister. They were chatting up a storm and admiring the colorful, beautiful flower garden. My dad was mellowing out and listening to jazz in the family room. I was like a thief in the night; I was busy placing the ladder beneath the attic door, and in a flash, I was climbing up like a little girl with a huge beige plastic bucket in one hand, and a large white cup inside the bucket. My plan was to use the cup to scoop up the water. The attic floor was made of thin plywood that softened like cardboard whenever it got damp, so I had always been careful not to step directly on it. Soon, I began my mission. I was busy scooping the water from the filled metal container into the bucket. The bucket was full, and without thinking, I stepped onto the damp attic floor instead of the wooden beam. Before I realized I had made a mistake, the floor collapsed and I burst through, flying in the air toward the garage below. There was a huge crashing sound as well as a big splash as the bucket broke into little pieces. There I was, coming silently through the air; I didn't make a sound. I remember thinking that this was a strange way for me to die. My eyes were open wide and I could see a small, bright light. It got larger and became brilliant, and it stopped in front of me. This was becoming bizarre, because it communicated with me in some strange telepathic way. It definitely was not verbal. I felt an intense love coming from the light. The light asked me if I wanted to go with it. I was confused, and a part of me wanted to. I felt like if I went with it, I would die. I said no softly, and the light began to recede. Then I saw my brother's face, with his smooth, dark, silky skin and enormous brown eyes. I felt an intense warmth surround me.

My brother was smiling as he tilted his head. At this point, I saw myself as I bounced on the edge of the car parked in the garage. Straight ahead was my mom, sliding in the water as she ran toward me, forming a cup with her hands. Everything was in slow motion, and my mom had an interesting look on her face. My head was just about to hit the concrete when my mom cupped my head with her big palms. She prevented the blow from happening. It was all so mystical and surreal. I broke four ribs and a pelvic bone. The paramedics were in awe that I was not in worse condition or dead from my thirteen-foot fall. Just then, the phone rang, and it was a call from Jamaica saying that my grandma had been admitted to the hospital. My parents had to return to Jamaica that same evening. By the end of the week, my grandma had passed away.

The possibility of an existence of life after death has always fascinated me. I am convinced now more than ever. I got a glimpse of it, not to mention that amazing feeling of peace that came over me. It was unlike anything else I have ever experienced in my life. I cannot forget my brother's radiant smile. It was surreal.

Daddy's Journey to a Beautiful Place

I never knew my dad to be sick while I was growing up. I rarely even saw him get a cold. I had a feeling that Daddy knew that he was becoming sick. He had become more sentimental in the last year before he got his diagnosis of colon cancer. He would whisper to me that he was going home soon. I would say to him, "Daddy, stop talking like that." Daddy wanted to see more of me in the last months even before the pain began. I cannot stop wondering if he knew and didn't want to say anything, because there must have been some signs. Jamaican men as a whole do not like going to see the doctor, and only God knows how long Daddy had the cancer inside him. I believe it must have been about twenty years. It is said that colon cancer is the silent killer, and now I know why. My parents retired in the United States for just four years so that they could be closer to my sister and me, and the grandchildren.

They planned to travel and enjoy some relaxing cruises, but that would never be the case.

When Daddy told us that he had a little pain in his right side, we didn't think anything much of it. We thought perhaps it was a problem with his appendix, so we insisted that he go see a doctor just to find out what was going on. From then on, everything went rapidly. It pained us to hear that Daddy received a diagnosis of stage four colon cancer. But even then, he was always optimistic. Not once did he feel sorry for himself. I spent every day of the last weeks with Daddy in the hospital. My dad looked at me one night while he was in the hospital and asked me for a pen and paper.

The next day he asked me, "Chirpie, please look in the top drawer of my bedside table at home, where you will find a mottled black-and-white notebook. You will know what to do." I did as he asked, and inside the notebook, found that my dad had written his autobiography, which took my breath away. He also had a plan of how he wanted his funeral to be. He had the Bible verses written out, plus the names of the officiating ministers, the organist, and very close friends he had had since his childhood whom he wanted to read his eulogy and remembrances. I was in awe.

My dad told me that he wanted me to read Psalm 121 from the King James Version:

> I will lift up mine eyes unto the hills, from whence cometh my help. My help cometh from the

LORD, which made heaven and earth. He will not suffer thy foot to be moved: he that keepeth thee will not slumber. Behold, he that keepeth Israel shall neither slumber nor sleep. The LORD is thy keeper: the LORD is thy shade upon thy right hand. The sun shall not smite thee by day, nor the moon by night.

The LORD shall preserve thee from all evil: he shall preserve thy soul. The LORD shall preserve thy going out and thy coming in from this time forth, and even forevermore.

I asked my dad, my eyes filled with tears, "Daddy, how will I find the strength to read this?"

He said, "Chirpie, you will. Just do not cry. You cannot cry."

"Daddy, that's impossible!" I said.

He just told me that he knew I would do a beautiful reading.

My dad wanted a memorial service here in the United States where he would lie in state, meaning his coffin would be placed on view so people could come by and pay their respects. Then he wanted to be cremated and have his ashes taken to his final resting place in Jamaica.

As the days went by, I would take weeks off from work to visit my dad in the hospital. I played sweet jazz music for Daddy that he loved so much, it made him smile, and

I told him that I loved him every chance I got. He told us that he had a few more days left, so one day, all the grandchildren went to the hospital to visit Daddy. They built a magnificent tower of their hands, beginning first with Daddy's hand, then one on top of the other. They expressed their love for him, each in their own way. The days to follow were serene and quiet.

We would break down at seeing him in pain at times, and he would simply say that it was all part of his journey. He told me that his journey had indeed begun, and that he was going to a beautiful place. He was so calm and peaceful. He was not scared to die. It was as though he knew something we didn't know. He was filled with anticipation about departing from this place that we call earth.

It was like a dream to me, and I actually compare it to being in an airport, destined to go on a fabulous tropical vacation, just waiting for the flight to be announced to board the airplane for departure. It was surreal!

He repeated to me at least a hundred times to be strong for Mommy. He was not worried at all about himself.

When Mommy told him that it was okay to let go now, he was gone in less than twenty-four hours. I knew he would pass away within a day of her telling him that, because he *always* valued her opinions, and she was the deciding factor in everything in his and their life. He had such remarkable strength, fortitude, and temperance. That was Daddy. And we will miss him very much. The day he passed, he looked as young as he looked in his wedding photograph. To top it all, he had a glowing Mona Lisa smile on his face.

The two memorial services were celebrations of Daddy's life.

I read the eulogy for my dad's memorial service. I was filled with the grace of God and felt my dad's presence. I was guided by a touch on my shoulder and I did it! I took one breath and read the eulogy with poise. I almost stumbled in a few areas, but my dad kept me going.

At the second celebration of life for Daddy in Jamaica, I read from the First Epistle of Peter 1:3–9.

Where will our focus re-form now? How do we maintain as a family, without our gravitational center? I guess we'll figure it out as we go along. I asked my dad during his last days, "Daddy, how will I know that you're with me when you are gone?"

My dad replied, "I will be with you in your dreams." He was right! Ever since he passed, he has been a guiding force for me through my dreams, and now I have a guardian angel. I am surrounded by love, light, and sound. If you desire love, you have to realize that the only way to get love is by giving love. The light is to show me what I must overcome, and the sound is for uplifting and strengthening my heart. He also said to me, "Chirpie, *never forget that love does not die because a loved one dies.*" I never knew that I would deal with the death of my dad the way I do now. I am sad because I miss him, but I am happy in another sense because he is in a beautiful place now, far beyond my imagination. I talk to my daddy sometimes too, especially when I am graced with his presence.

I remember my dad telling me that everyone is a divine being who comes to life on earth with a spiritual purpose, and that his purpose in life was to find his way back home to God.

I will never forget his precious words. My dad will always remain to me the person I hope someday to become.

That's the world my dad saw.

This was his life.

Any man can be a FATHER, but it takes someone special to be a DAD!

I have included a marriage-proposal letter that my dad wrote to my grandma, asking her for my mom's (Hope-Honey) hand in marriage, just to give you a taste of the kind of old-fashioned gentleman that my dad was.

P.O. Box 256,
Montego Bay, St. James,
Jamaica
February 3, 1962

Lethel, my Darling Mother,

May your life be filled with pleasantness, with love and friendship true, more blessed with health and happiness and good things all for you.

This letter is to formally ask your daughter's hand in marriage. I love Honey very dearly, and wish to share peace, happiness and my entire life with her. Hope is a phantom of delight when first she gleamed upon my sight; a lovely apparition sent to be a moments armament, a perfect woman nobly planned to warm, to comfort and command, and yet a spirit still and bright with something of an angel light.

I have known Honey since 1953, and have always admired her from thence; however, not revealing my love for her until 1957. We love each other very earnestly and with every breath of air I take; every thought my mind creates, Honey is foremost amidst and amongst them. I love her as no man ever loved a woman and feel quite capable to make her comfortable and happy living with me.

Warm friendship like the constant sun sheds kindly rays on everyone; it warms the heart and brings a smile and makes us feel life is worthwhile.

My greatest desire and pleasure would be to take care of Hope in the role of husband, companion, and lover. There is no companion where love and friendship stands faithful. Happiness is not a possession to be prized, but a quality of thought, a state of mind. Respectability, honesty, and sincerity is what I yearn for, and the path that a man ought to choose is that which honors him in his own eyes and makes him worthy of respect to the eyes of others.

Lethel Mother, wilt thou accept me as your loving son-in-law, to love, to respect, honor and care for Hope? I promise to do all in my power to make Hope the happiest woman in the world, to minimize as much as possible misunderstandings which may arise from time to time in married life.

Honey has made it very clear to me that she will, without further postponement, be my wife to cherish. Please give us your blessings in this matter and allow me the happiness of taking good care of your daughter.

You have always been sweet to me and I must congratulate you on being the mother of the most darling girl I have known. She has qualities that I greatly admire, and her physical beauty is to me, beyond compare. I see in her most of everything that I have desired and do covet of a wife. She surely can bring joy, happiness, and love to my life, and so will make it my vow to keep her far from harm's way.

It is a good thing to give thanks unto the Lord and to sing praises unto the name of the moist high. My mouth shall speak of wisdom and the meditation of my heart shall be of understanding.

Let not your heart be troubled, as being with me, honey will be cared for, and no harm shall come to her. I shall love, preserve, cherish, and try to understand her in all things to the will of God, so please accept my proposition of son-in-law to you, and, husband to your daughter Hope.

Behold how good and how pleasant it is for brethren to dwell together in unity.

Yours always,
Yorke

A Special Rainbow for My Dad

By Angela Brent-Harris

Daddy will always be in my mind and in my heart,

That's why I decided to paint him a rainbow, and here's where I'll start.

I'll begin on a canvas of warm memories, patience, warmth, and love,

I'll continue with spirituality and inner peace from heaven above.

On a palette of kind words I tenderly will blend

Rich tones of compassion, and calmness that will never end.

They'll glow with sincerity and blessings galore.

My daddy's the person that I'll always adore.

I'll paint colors of sweet dreams, happiness, and laughter,

Knowing we'll meet again in the life hereafter.

For in the depth of the center of each different hue,

Warm love, a memory fashioned for Daddy so true.

Me

By Angela Brent-Harris

I have to know *me* and love me and live with *me,*

And be in good health and let the blessings be.

I want to look in the mirror at myself eye to eye,

And be content with who I am, and it's sure worth a try.

I don't want to stare at the setting sun and ponder and fret

On things I have or haven't done, even on deadlines that are not met.

I want to walk with a smile, chin up with my head erect,

And to be able to be deserving of all men's respect.

I will not hide myself from me,

I see what others may never see.

I want to laugh, skip around, and sometimes be carefree.

The life really is too short, I am happy to be me.

Quotes

———◆———

Life is short, so keep it sweet! Try to think of good things—happy, kind, and helpful thoughts. Then your life can be filled with contentment, because there will be no space left for unkindness to fill in your mind. Life is what your thoughts make it to be.

—Angela Brent-Harris

Be happy with who you are. Love yourself. The secret of happiness is in recognizing your own flaws and strengths. Find fulfillment in a direction of your potential, and the ability to face being your own genuine person, without wanting to be someone else!

—Angela Brent-Harris

Do not worry about what people say about you. Instead, spend your time trying to achieve something that will gain their respect and approval.

—Angela Brent-Harris

Allow Your Inner Light to Guide You

There comes a time when you must stand alone.
You must feel confident enough within
yourself to follow your own dreams.
You must be willing to make sacrifices.
You must be capable of changing and rearranging your
priorities so that your final goal can be achieved.
Sometimes, familiarity and comfort
need to be challenged.
There are times when you must take a few extra
chances and create your own realities.
Be strong enough to at least try to make your life better.
Be confident enough that you won't settle
for a compromise just to get by.

Appreciate yourself by allowing yourself

the opportunities to grow, develop,

and find your true sense of

Purpose in this life.

Don't stand in someone else's shadow when

it's your sunlight that should lead the way.

— www.indianchild.com

Open Book Editions
A Berrett-Koehler Partner

Open Book Editions is a joint venture between Berrett-Koehler Publishers and Author Solutions, the market leader in self-publishing. There are many more aspiring authors who share Berrett-Koehler's mission than we can sustainably publish. To serve these authors, Open Book Editions offers a comprehensive self-publishing opportunity.

A Shared Mission

Open Book Editions welcomes authors who share the Berrett-Koehler mission—Creating a World That Works for All. We believe that to truly create a better world, action is needed at all levels—individual, organizational, and societal. At the individual level, our publications help people align their lives with their values and with their aspirations for a better world. At the organizational level, we promote progressive leadership and management practices, socially responsible approaches to business, and humane and effective organizations. At the societal level, we publish content that advances social and economic justice, shared prosperity, sustainability, and new solutions to national and global issues.

Open Book Editions represents a new way to further the BK mission and expand our community. We look forward to helping more authors challenge conventional thinking, introduce new ideas, and foster positive change.

For more information, see the Open Book Editions website: http://www.iuniverse.com/Packages/OpenBookEditions.aspx

Join the BK Community! See exclusive author videos, join discussion groups, find out about upcoming events, read author blogs, and much more! http://bkcommunity.com/

CPSIA information can be obtained at www.ICGtesting.com
Printed in the USA
BVOW03s1900060314

346906BV00001B/36/P